FIRST MANUSCRIPT

INGENIUM AWAKENING

THE CODEX OF

CHARACTER ETIQUETTE

Chahrazade Belamine

Written by Chahrazade Belamine

UK July 2023

All Rights Reserved.

Limits of liability and disclaimer of warranty.

The purpose of this book is to educate. The author and/or publisher shall have neither liability nor responsibility to anyone, with respect to any damage caused, or alleged to be caused, directly or indirectly, by the information contained in this book.

TABLE OF CONTENTS

Table of contents	6
About the title	10
Dedication	12
Preface	15
Introduction	16
1. Aim to become a person of value	18
2. Embody a set of values	22
3. Speak your truth	26
4. Be true to your word	30
5. Become loyal	32
6. Be well mannered	35
7. Be grateful	38
8. Cultivate eloquence	42
9. Mind your speech	46
10. Learn to listen	52
11. Mind your body language	60
12. Receive gracefully	62
13. Give generously	68

14. Be clean and orderly	71
15. Declutter your space	74
16. Be well organized	77
17. Be productive	79
18. Be mindful of your time	80
19. Develop self-discipline	84
20. Aim for completion	87
21. Be savvy	88
22. Seek knowledge	90
23. Grow mindset clarity	93
24. Show professionalism	95
25. Know respect	98
26. Cultivate the right culture	100
27. Be a good role model	102
28. Be responsible	111
29. Be presentable	112
30. Be agreeable	115
31. Practice self-control	118
32. Sharpen your saw	121
33. Develop charisma	122
34. Know thyself	125

35. Live the present	127
36. Change yourself first	131
37. Be forgiving	133
38. Be authentic	139
39. Be loving	141
40. Be non-judgmental	147
41. Be vulnerable	149
42. Be assertive	153
43. Plan and prepare	155
44. Be bold	157
45. Become fit	160
46. Eat well	163
47. Hydrate yourself	168
48. Practice self-care	172
49. Find time for detox	175
50. Do quality time	177
51. Feel good	179
52. Avoid wastage	181
53. Intention matters	184
54. Enter a sacred union	186
55. Raise a family	189

56. Nourish your inner circle	195
57. Practice mindfulness	196
58. Heal your wounds	198
59. Nurture your aura	206
60. Experience divine energy	208
61. Heavenly realm	210
62. About manifestation	212
Conclusion	216

ABOUT THE TITLE

Writing is an inspired gift that came about a decade ago and this fresh poetic prose comes to complement the spiritual pen journey.

As a Sorbonne University graduate with Latin rudiments and deep spiritual inclination, my questioning mind has sought and studied religions, scriptures and related topics for many years. To this day, I enjoy the layered reading of the divine message.

The title reflects a divine related essay, aimed at portraying a complete being, endowed with character, intellect, value-based thinking, physical strength and in-flow spirit.

The content is a verbiage ramble in direct prose and symbolic poetry, enriched with scriptural quotes, thus orating a literary architecture.

INGENIUM in Latin means genius, innate quality, embedded character, nature, disposition, temper, intelligence, inclination, ability, art and in Medieval Latin, it refers to a machine or an engine.

AWAKENING as a verb form is an action with the meaning of awakening from sleep, becoming aware, coming into existence, experiencing a revival that can be spiritually related.

CODEX is an ancient manuscript in book form with a scriptural innuendo.

(Implied GOOD) CHARACTER is the embodiment of praiseworthy traits, values and virtues that promote goodness and wellbeing.

ETIQUETTE is the embellishment of social human behavior with a customary code of good manners and courtesy.

DEDICATION

I dedicate this heart centered book to my family and loved ones.

With Love,

Chahrazade Belamine

For the Know Thyself seeker,

Consciously aware & eager,

Working at awakening,

Higher version of being,

Multidimensional era,

Human character aura,

Mind spark luminescent,

Body made efficient,

High vibrational spirit,

In service, divine gift.

PREFACE

This book came after an interruption in my writing journey. For weeks, home, family and work duties filled my diary. Suddenly, the inspired quill stood up and gathered words in a new composition...

The topic in mind was character reform.

I have indeed come to the realization that scriptural teachings do advocate character reform, self-empowerment and active faith contribution.

With life experience, one comes to realise what really matters, which traits of character stand out, which principles are worthwhile and what positively influences society and human interactions.

In the spiritual quest for the purpose of life, the souls, seeking self-realization, uncover the God-given gifts they can share with the world. Those light bearers enlighten it, expand it and inspire collective growth.

An important topic such as character building encompasses many aspects and I hope that this book will unravel the potential greatness of human character.

INTRODUCTION

As per the title, this book aims to draw attention to the epitome of a noble character and refined manners.

The scriptural teachings emphasize how righteousness must be sought and how goodness is an essential element of character development.

Your character, mindset, heart and behavior reflect your personal identity. You choose to decide in this life how you wish to influence your inner circle and define your role in society.

Here are some questions to ask yourself.

Who is my role model (or role models)?

Who would I like to emulate?

Which traits do they possess?

What values do they uphold?

How do they contribute?

What impact do I want to have in this world?

This book is an invitation in prose and poetry to consider praiseworthy aspects of human character.

It might trigger a quest to embody the best version of yourself.

1/ AIM TO BECOME A PERSON OF VALUE

A major aspect of human experience relates to finding your life purpose. On the path to this journey of discovery, the array of gifts that you bring to the world is unleashed.

You might ask yourself and wonder about the I? What am I good at? What are the skills that I acquire easily? What are the things that I do better than others? What do I incline towards? What discoveries, expertise and accomplishments can I or do I bring to the world?

This facet of societal contribution derives from the learning experience that one acquires via lineage, childhood, environment, parents, teachers, social circle, networking, training, education, hands-on experience, etc. and it can be triggered externally or internally. What do I mean by that?

The finding of your gifts can come via an inspired action, an occurrence, a thought, an idea, a coincidental encounter, an a-ha moment, a trial-and-error experimentation, a discovery of a gap in the market, an entrepreneurial venture, a futuristic thought (specifically in the case of inventors and pioneers), a problem-solving solution, a belief-based motivation, a philanthropic action or an incentive to leave a legacy and the list goes on.

Often, it seems that our own experience of healing, recovery, awakening, transformation becomes the trigger to help and inspire others. As you discover your own gifts and release them into the world, you help others to do the same.

As you find yourself, more follow suit.

Perfection is not a prerequisite. It is rather the striving for excellence in your field of knowledge and expertise that is required.

The mastery of a topic and subject matter is confirmed by your own personal achievement and accreditation via learning and practical experimentation. Learning is not limited to the theoretical level and rather the practical aspect of thinking, living and doing.

How do you know that you are endowed with a gift or even several?

This is often referred to as "being in the flow." The activity is mastered with effortless mastery and dexterity. The gifted master is equipped with a built-in confidence in the topic that compliments the skillful action. Successful historical figures, artists and athletes are a good example of high-level mastery.

How can you discover your abilities?

Regular self-assessment is useful to identify your preferences and inclinations, followed by efforts to develop those areas. Experimenting various tasks, environments, contexts, people and activities is quite helpful to discover yourself. As you realise what you are good at and what you enjoy doing, you find that with practice, you can attain mastery in such field of expertise.

Every skill is learnable.

A conscious achievement is built with strong will, laser focus, solid mindset, motivation and perseverance. With 'practice makes perfect' formula, the gradual experimentation transforms itself.

The subject mastery is a gift when it is intrinsically congruent and authentic to your core being. It is comparable to an innate quality.

Decide to serve,

Honor in deserve,

Share with society,

Wit & skill ability,

True gift master,

Work endeavor,

Live for a reason,

Shine light beacon,

Find your meaning,

O you, spiritual being!

2/ EMBODY A SET OF VALUES

What might distinguish one person from another is the set of human values that one stands for.

Having a benchmark of values equates to distinguishing what matters, according to the selected criterion. Therefore, it is important to select values that are relevant to you and abide by them. Not only does it provide guidance in decision making, but also a reliable referential for life. Those values can relate to some or all aspects of living.

Typically, those principles can stem from religious references, lineage, social protocol, family, culture, objective morality, humanity, common sense and personal choice.

The value compass provides a referential benchmark and a behavioral foundation.

When you stand by high quality values, you possess discernment and guidance.

To discover your values, recall the times when you were the happiest and when you were most proud and fulfilled. Those moments often symbolize the important aspects of life that you hold dear.

Once you have identified what is truly relevant in your human experience, create your selection benchmark.

Raw Values in Rhyme Rambles

Authenticity in your reality,

Adventure, a great venture,

Balance, sports, dance,

Compassion & dedication,

Challenge at risk range,

Citizenship & craftmanship,

Community & solidarity,

Creativity & artistry,

Curiosity in quirky,

Determination in action,

Fairness in entireness,

Freedom arboretum,

Friendships tight knits,

Fun, joke & laughter,

Generosity, magnanimity,

Growth & regrowth,

Honesty & decency,

Integrity, equanimity,

Justice & humanity,

Kindness, lovingness,

Knowledge acumen pledge,

Leadership & fellowship,

Learning & discovering,

Love & beloved,

Loyalty & sincerity,

Openness & frankness,

Optimism & idealism,

Recognition & realization,

Respect, ranks, reverence,

Responsibility & reliability,

Security & safety,

Self-respect & etiquette,

Social connection & relation,

Spirituality & divinity,

Stability & constancy,

Status, roles, credentials,

                                        Wealth, estates, assets,

Wisdom, radiance, sapience.

Equipped with a set of beliefs and a value benchmark, your thought and behavioral process complies accordingly.

In fact, selecting personal, business and company values is an inherent part of strategic branding and marketing. It creates a reliable criterion for discernment and decision making, a relatable referential for target audience, a focused management compass and actions in alignment.

3/ SPEAK YOUR TRUTH

The topic of truth needs to be defined depending on the domain we address.

On the one hand, there is an objective truth, such as the obvious collective reality that we can all agree upon. Humans are having a sensorial experience on planet Earth. There is a spatial, temporal and dimensional awareness. There are mathematical and geometrical references.

On the other hand, there are subjective truths which relate to your human experience and personal perception of the world.

The subjective truth is linked to your brain conditioning during your cellular growth and life experience. We all perceive the world based on our beliefs and thoughts. This perception is conditioned by the effect of our human experience.

For instance, you might recall a memorable experience that influenced you and it resulted in a new way of thinking. Or, you might have experienced a certain mood or feeling that altered your world perception and you now behave differently.

To that extent, I will define speaking your truth by being truthful and congruent with who you are.

Speaking truthfully is the vocal aspect of expressing your real beliefs and convictions.

When you are truthful, it happens in the time and space moment. Your intention is to tell the truth. You mean the words you utter. Your action matches your speech. You are consciously congruent.

Now whether that truth might evolve later is another matter. At the time of utterance, its reality is authentic.

Sincerity also relates to your benchmark of values. When being truthful is an acknowledged principle, then you are authentic in yourself.

Your being in alignment shows no discrepancy in speech, thought and behavior. You are authentically congruent with your true self.

Truth is applicable in the array of human communication.

Beyond speech eloquent,

Raw truth statement,

Artistical expression,

Skilled art of motion,

Exquisite painting,

Intricate drawing,

Shivering musical,

Song tune recital,

Heartfelt poetry,

Sync choreography,

Well-crafted piece,

Sculpted masterpiece,

Chef signature dish,

Top salesman pitch,

Pioneer architect,

Clever intellect,

Athletic master,

Inspiring teacher,

Chess strategist,

Wonderful artist,

Scientist discovery,

Surgeon mastery,

Lawyer court compelling,

Detective eye sharpening,

Thorough researcher,

Innovative inventor,

The devoted passionate,

The excellency of great,

The sublime learned,

The spiritually guided.

4/ BE TRUE TO YOUR WORD

This is the quality that makes a positive impact around you as it reflects your truthfulness as a person.

When you keep your word, it means that your meaningful words translate into relatable actions.

It is a sign of reliability and a conscious ability in your speech to become a reality. The word that is meant and uttered at a specific moment has a weight in value that is confirmed by the action that follows.

It does not mean that you cannot change your mind, but rather that what you promise does become a reality practically.

Delivering on a spoken word or promise is not only beneficial in the love and social context, but also in the work arena and in teamwork when tasks are delegated accordingly.

It equates to the simplified command:

'DO WHAT YOU SAY YOU ARE GOING TO DO'.

> **Bible, Ecclesiastes 5.5** It is better not to make a vow than to make one and not fulfill it.

Standing by your word is a noble attribute that typically illustrates a high value character.

To be word worthy is a superior trait.

A thoughtful speech that becomes a reality is impactful, even more relevant when a command, a promise or an oath is made.

Scripturally, the Word (in Greek 'Logos') is often referred to as the foundation of the divine and the divinely inspired action.

> **Bible, John 1.1** In the beginning was the Word, and the Word was with God, and the Word was God.

5/ BECOME LOYAL

I would initially refer to self-loyalty, which is typically congruency and adherence to your own belief system.

Loyalty to your selected criteria equates to a logical life methodology.

For instance, if punctuality is an important value for me, I apply it first before expecting it from others.

I aim to keep loyal to my set of beliefs and values as long as I adhere to that belief and value.

If loyalty to a person is a key aspect of your character, then it constantly reflects on your relationship with your loved ones. It might even extend to other areas of your life.

While it is praiseworthy to uphold your own values, it is important to acknowledge the difference. In a world of diversity, we know that our fellow brethren might have divergent beliefs and values.

Loyalty is a gift because having a loyal spouse, a loyal friend, a loyal worker, etc. provides a healthy trust foundation.

Loyalty is to acknowledge and prioritize the status of that criteria, whether it is with yourself or your loved ones.

Loyalty breeds reliability in the sense that you know whom you can rely on, and it is usually discovered in tough times.

Obviously, in war strategy, loyalty is typically undermined by the enemy to weaken the united foundation.

Loyalty breeds transparency,
Communication, mindset clarity,

It is not a taken for granted token,
But mutual esteem, a bonding den,

A relationship of like-minded,
Sharing values, goals guided,

Loyalty strengthening character,
Social & friendship thermometer,

Amazing unwavering loyalty,
Bonded reward, accordingly,

Loyalty stems in prophethood,

Companionship, knighthood,

                                        Allegiance-based royalty,
                                          Group, sect, community,

                   Anointed ones especially,
                   Divine blessing nobility.

6/ BE WELL MANNERED

Good manners beautify a person, an action or a situation.

Social courtesy can be culturally relevant and adapted to the contextual time and space. Different nations have specific behavioral etiquette.

Politeness is globally recognized, and noble manners embellish and sweeten relationships and business transactions.

First, good manners are a code of etiquette within the cultural context. Politeness and courtesy are inherent to the etiquette benchmark.

The normalization of 'please' and 'thank you' is the simplified version as it extends way beyond that.

A polite way of formally and informally greeting someone is typically by speech, eye contact, physical movement or touch (bow, nod, handshake, kiss), and attentiveness.

Noble manners include the art of communication and social etiquette. In essence, it is the act of presence in front of your fellow humans.

For instance, it may include greeting, welcoming, introducing, mindful talking, attentive listening, not interrupting and courteous adapting to the socio-cultural context. It also means upholding the tokens of thankfulness, gratefulness, consideration and appreciation.

Considerate social behavior is usually bred by a good education and positive role modeling.

The expansion of good manners in the gender field typically relates to masculine gallantry and feminine appreciation.

At times of courtship,
The gentleman Lordship,
Would open door bravely,
Be mindful intelligently,

Take matters at hand,
Respectful in command,
Mastering the pathway,
Walking the right way,

A provider mentality,
Supporting constantly,
A warrior defending,
Vulnerable protecting,

The mastered gallantry,
Such courteous chivalry.

                          The Lady would captivate,
                          And lovingly appreciate,
                          The masculine approach,
                          Enhancing the coach,

A feline in loving,
A mother in raising,
A feminine Goddess,
A divine enchantress.

Nowadays, with the rise of technology, sexual expression and liberalization, gender titles and roles have been blurred. Women and men have both taken on each other roles, tasks and responsibilities.

For those upholding traditional values, gallantry is relevant and remarkably refreshing in expressing the yin and yang energy.

7/ BE GRATEFUL

There is no doubt that acquiring a mindset of gratefulness is worthwhile as it brings peace and contentment.

The ebb and flow of life enables the appreciation of creation. With the understanding of cyclical polarity comes the knowing of what is wonderful, beneficial, loving, constructive and strikingly beautiful.

Be a thankful soul,

O you layered shawl,

Gratefulness feeds appreciation,
See the wrong, devise a solution,

Know human flaw & quality thread,
Live your experiential story ahead,

Enjoy the countless blessings granted,

Cherish the moment and take heed,

> *Delight at the spectacular creation,*
> *Awaken to the superb sensation,*

Rise and heighten emotion,
Perceive self-realization,

> *With such an awakening,*
> *Comes a radiant being.*

Gratefulness is an essential quality. It transforms your perception of life and makes you realise what is valuable.

The simple act of breathing and having a sensorial experience on this Earth is mind blowing.

Being able to feed your heart and mind with the knowledge of appreciation requires practice. Somehow, there is a human tendency to dwell on what is or what went wrong. Complaining is an unrequited habit. A deliberate switch to focus on what is right elevates the mind into problem solving and thankfulness.

Mindful contemplation raises the sense of awe and amazement at the miracles of creation.

Fresh young minds wander,
Delight enchanting wonder,

Unconscious exhilaration,
Awe reverent passion,

The innocence of purity,
In happiness worry-free,

Skillful in imagination,
Resourceful in creation,

Joyful mindset at play,
In bewitching disarray,

Then come responsibility,

Burdens mind agility,

Remember the dreamland,
Starry sky, sea and sand,

Gardens of heavenly,
Paradisical reality,

Everything is possible,
Mind willing and able,

Heartfelt tremendously,
Sensational ingenuity,

Miraculous living,
Deep soul inspiring.

8/ CULTIVATE ELOQUENCE

Gracious gait of eloquence,
Layered meanings' trance,

A highly skilled orator,
A speech exquisite actor,

Thoughts and ideas,
Dance in musical ears,

Articulated artfully,
Well-sought excellency,

Captivating audience,
Mastering presence,

Movements on stage,
Interactively engage,

The crowd speechless,
Puzzled, God bless,

        Skins are shivering,
        Emotion rise bonding

                The rhythmic intensity,
                Hype the reactivity,

A jubilant applaud,
Feedback the reward,

        Vibrational matching,
        Intentional appealing,

                The atmosphere electric,
                Spell charisma magnetic.

Excellence in communication, whilst adapting to the contextual audience, is a high value skill.

Consciously selecting your words, tuning your vocal notes, adjusting your tone, practicing pauses, and adapting your speech flow require practice.

The expression of speech is as meaningful as its delivery and content.

Breathing techniques, tone variations, pauses, voice pitches and speed are the rhythmic elements of vocal expression.

The choice of words and semantics, well-formed sentences, depictive adjectives, prose and poetry compose the form of the speech.

The speaker's aim is for the listener to understand the elocution and the emphasized ideas. The core message is to be retained.

Onstage performance is the physical aspect of message delivery that is expressed via sitting, standing, walking, hands and body movements.

The intensity of energy transfer, shared passion, aroused feelings and sensations create the emotional impact of a discourse.

The speech methodology relates to how the information is presented.

The elocution can be illustrated with facts, numbers, stories, jokes, statements, metaphors, similes, metaphors, parables, analogies, examples, rhetorical questions, concise or detailed information, references and when applicable, supported with audio visual aids.

The right message is transmitted with a communication medium adapted to the relevant audience for optimal expression and understanding.

Concise audio and visually curated messages are perfect for a social media platform while a more academic and elaborate delivery form is ideal for a teaching module.

Eloquence also relates to how you express yourself.

Unless you are with someone highly skilled in mind reading and emotional intelligence, it is essential to know how to express your own wants, desires, feelings, thoughts, goals, expectations, ideas, teachings, etc.

Speech eloquence also relies on the non-verbal cues as 80% of our communication is non-verbal. Your body speech and energy radiation accompany the verbal transmission.

The speech should be an extension of the communication model formed by our emotions, energetic blueprint and body expression.

9/ MIND YOUR SPEECH

Less is more when talking,
Brief words, perfect timing,

        Impulsive emotion rushing,
        A heart-felt talk is coming,

                Sharp speech magnet,
                Synchronicity outlet,

Disregard enragement,
Dismiss discouragement,

        Rant, complain, nag bite,
        Scornful critic, backbite,

                Hate, hit, argue, swearing,
                Woe to those not enticing!

Spreading encouragement,
Voice to build the moment,

      Words can heal the listener,
      O eloquent righteous speaker,

            Joined words in collaboration,
            Support, help, recommendation,

Romantic script, heart loving,
Words of passion unravelling,

      Lectures guiding, teaching,
      Management and advising,

            Expert spread influence,
            Speak & inspire confidence,

Words breed transformation,
High consciousness elevation.

Words stem from letters,
Words are perfect orators,

Words scramble in creation,
Words impact self-realization,

Words power weights in motion,
Words mirror state of imagination,

Words are clever instruments of chi,
Words can elevate your mood energy,

Words are rooted in the love language,
Words of essence carry divine message.

Mind your speech brew,
Blend words, bring value,

Develop seductive know-how,
Compose musical intelligentsia,

Shy, bothered, grab attention,
Energize tone, feed expression,

Silent pause, timed communication,
So much to say rush in vocalization.

Fast, clever, creative and fiery,
Think quick, brainstorming fury,

Sophisticated talk captivating,
Power words rhythmic moving,

A well-crafted speech intensity,
Spoken and articulated clearly,

    Energy speaks magnetism,
    Charisma lures hypnotism,

        Mind delights literacy,
        Such impactful delivery.

10/ LEARN TO LISTEN

Listening is an art sport,
Everyone likes to gloat,

                I, I and the ego.
                Interrupt convo lingo,

                              Babble and blabber,
                              Rant rattle clever,

          Dialoguing, monologuing?
          Boring or interesting?

Discuss bright ideas.
Tell jokes or stories.

Expressive thoughts,

Illustrating anecdotes,

Observing, listening,

Teaching and learning.

Attend the world swirl,
Can you hear the twirl?

God and the Universe,
Cosmic Earth converse,

Living things moving,
Animals, trees talking,

Plants, fungus fidgeting,
Biodiversity interacting,

Rocks, water enlivening,
Weather participating,

Soil, sky, sea, sun,
Planets' orbit run,

Sense inner intention,

Insightful intuition,

Smart anticipation,

Deciphering emotion,

Mind chatter chatting,

Heart language loving,

Body vibes signaling,

Soul intense revealing.

The dialogue of energy exchange,
A mutually shared experience,

                        A mindful talking stance,
                        Artful listening presence,

                                            Are you attentive?
                                            Do you perceive?

Apply full attention,
Ears tuning,
Hearts bonding,
Minds joining,
Souls linking.

The body speaks incredibly,
Cosmic machine of energy,

        Brazing eyes conversing,
        Unravel the surrounding,

                Red lips read even shut,
                Taste buds smiling hut,

Moody verbal literacy,
Crunch life exquisitely,

        Delicatessen flavor spicy,
        Fruit exotic ethnic fiery,

                Perfume fragrance enticing,
                Mixed notes exhilarating,

Textures and fabrics waving,
The finger touch wandering,

Moves reveal undoubtedly,
Body silk craze curiosity,

Heartfelt emotion instantly,
Gut feeling sense reality,

Wave motion of vibration,
Electric charged interaction,

Cosmic realm entering,
Eternity field hugging,

Apex stillness tension,
Overpowering emotion,

Epic conscious presence,

Divine omnipresence.

Body expression can show attentiveness.

Indications of good listening behavior consist of participation, engagement, concentrated eyes, an inclined body, attentive ears, a smile or nod, stillness, and receptivity.

Examples of social communication techniques include mirroring body language, paraphrasing, requesting clarification, probing, asking open-ended questions, using brief affirmations, empathizing and sharing similar experiences.

11/ MIND YOUR BODY LANGUAGE

Body language carries an energy signature and illustrates a character trait.

A dynamic gait shows an energetic person.

A cheerful countenance indicates a happy, smiley and receptive character.

Speaking clearly with open arms illustrates a warm and confident person.

Behavior in social situations can indicate the type of person in that moment: introvert or extrovert, loud or quiet, participant or observant, alone or in group, rude or courteous, casual or smart, funny or serious, etc.

Body language speaks beyond words.

It reflects the person's state and energy blueprint.

Changing your body language can help alter your internal state.

States can vary according to personal context and circumstances.

When you are aware of your body, you can lift your condition accordingly.

You might notice that when you slouch, you are either tired, laid back or relaxed.

Walking head and shoulders down indicates shyness, depression, low energy or avoidance and it limits your peripheral vision.

As per the lines of Jordan Peterson, standing straight and fixing your shoulders will make you feel better. An upright body posture displays confidence, good posture and enhances panoramic vision.

Often, behavioral posture comes from acquired habits, repeated actions or even the furniture structure. Examples might include extensive seating while working on a computer, writing on a table or bed in an unusual body position, laying on a soft mattress or sofa, seating on a low back chair, etc.

Physical behavior can also be cultural. In hot countries, laid back speech, leisurely walking, a relaxed work rhythm, slow days and late nights are living effects of the scorching heat.

Character, lineage, family, social rank and religious guidelines can also dictate social behavior and comportment.

12/ RECEIVE GRACEFULLY

The Latin root word of the word receive, *'recipere'*, has the meaning of making whole again.

In the hospitality industry, it relates to the etiquette of hosting a guest, whether in dining, entertaining or in accommodation.

The art of receiving is an integral part of good manners, courtesy and politeness. Some cultures are well renowned for their art of hospitality.

The hosting and dining in social circles can be relaxed, informal or formal, depending on the context, guest list and event.

The art of welcoming is linked to character development as it might include learning the "know how."

Be a great host skillfully,

Arrange events socially,

Excel at presentations,

Make proper introductions,

Sit guests appropriately,
Be attentive, courteously,

Prepare a menu full on,
Cook elaborated luncheon,

Set a refined table dining,
And hot topic conversing,

Crack a joke smiling,
Master the storytelling,

Dress with panache, elegance,
Groomed, polished appearance,

Mind conscious socially,
Interacting intelligently.

Hosting is a crafted art,

Social gathering smart,

        The flair of welcoming,
        The grace of receiving.

Are you receiving?

THE

Art of living,
Joy of loving,
Eyes gazing,
Lips smiling,
Heart beaming,
Moment stirring,

Union sight,
Soul ignite,
Touch alight,
Skin delight,
Craze insight,
Heavenly night,

Present mindful,
Cheering thankful,

Lover hopeful,
Friend helpful,
Soul peaceful,
World blissful,

Amicable hand,
Gift eloquent,
Sincere compliment,
Constructive comment,
Raw nature exuberant,
Cosmos grandiloquent,

Emotional time,
Challenging climb,
Successful prime,
Mature design,
Grace of a lifetime.
Spiritual sublime.

The flow cycle is lively,
Motion sense of energy,
Give receive gracefully
Awe-brilliant artistry.

13/ GIVE GENEROUSLY

To donate generously comes from an abundant mind.

Spirit luxuriant,
Mind effervescent,

        Love overflowing,
        Magnet fascinating,

                Ebullient riches, abundance,
                Radiate your donation expanse,

Gift of a heart loving,
Time, tip, lesson, feeling,

        Food, love, joyful moment,
        Hope, help, encouragement,

Words of advice, wealth besides,
Prayers, supplications & good vibes,

Donate without ostentation,
Bestow willingly an invitation,

Give as you would be recipient,
Blessed your courtesy beneficent,

Provide a bespoke service perfectly,
Shower personalized gifts intently,

Spread and share, love increasing,
Make contribution, society fulfilling,

Donate, feel the proud achievement,
Present an offering, purposeful remitment,

Dedicate an intention, volunteer sincerely,

Grow inner fulfilment, enrich humanity.

14/ BE CLEAN AND ORDERLY

While it is obvious that cleanliness is an inherent part of a well-dressed home, cleanliness can also be applied to mind, body, heart, soul and space.

The cleansing route is self-introspection and assessment.

Cleanliness encompasses inner and outer purification with environmental care.

Emptying the mind, cleansing the heart, minding the thoughts and washing the body parts are essential elements to maintain and nurture wellbeing.

Mind cleansing is about acquiring beneficial knowledge, converting negative thoughts into positive ones, being consciously mindful and thinking productively.

Physical cleansing implies water washing for energy reinvigoration plus daily grooming practices. It extends to daily hygiene, self-care, body washing, prepping and dressing with clean clothing.

Heart cleansing is about character reformation, managing emotions and acknowledging and replacing negative traits with constructive behavior.

Soul cleansing refers to spiritual practices like prayer, meditation, spiritual communion, mindfulness and contemplation.

Ensuring that the home is scrubbed on a regular basis is a foundation to home making. Cleaning can be done by the family members or the cleaners to achieve a clean and tidy home.

A crisp home is refreshed with daily ventilation, room fragrance and fresh flowers.

A pristine home makes sense as it provides clarity and well-being.

Cleaning stems from early good habits and effective time management.

As an extension to cleanliness, tidiness is about giving everything its place. Practically, when things are where they are supposed to be, everything is located quickly. Putting things close to their usage location makes more sense.

While it is known that managed chaos can breed creativity, it is essential to keep some order routine in the home.

Cleanliness and order in a home breeds wellbeing, focus and good energy.

There are many layers of cleaning,

Work, home and space dusting,
Filtering sensory bloodstream,
Sieving thought data stream,

Manage embedded traits,
Impress the better states,
Repel evil and negative,
Do good, be constructive,

Cleansed heart emotional,
Character mode beneficial,
Transform energy footprint,
Enlightened vibe blueprint,

Peeled layers of conditioning,
Ingenium mind unravelling,
A quest for soul equilibrium,
Yin & Yang sing harmonium.

15/ DECLUTTER YOUR SPACE

Decluttering is a healthy habit to acquire.

Regular spring cleaning is essential to refresh space energy, seasonal clothing and bedding. Cosmetics, perfumes, skin care, cupboard food, outgrown clothes, shoes and possessions need regular fixing or updating. The change of seasons provides an opportunity to do this quarterly home refresh.

In modern society, acquiring material possessions can lead to an excess of matter that becomes static energy when left unused. This is why moving furniture and objects, cleaning and tidying regularly affect the vigor of the home.

Doing an inventory of what you own is the starting point for the realization of the material impact.

Chase for the next purchase,

Fill a space at crazy pace,

Is matter only matter in creation?

Are we cumulative accumulation?

Mindless scrolling in little screen,

Machine wins in-between spleen,

Guess the eternal human quest,
Overcoming own self conquest,

Lighten the cumbersome burden,
Rise and rise again certain,

Feel the heart light revealing,
Hasten the soul awakening,

See beyond seeming reality,
Unravel marvel realm beauty.

There is a psychological dimension to excessively hoarding possessions.

It can be linked to asserting status, fearing lack, emotionally surrounding yourself with accompanying things, holding onto unprocessed emotions and post traumatic reactions.

Displaying material things and excessive riches can be the mere enjoyment of extreme abundance to forever override the survival mode.

From a design point of view, each home is unique and should be personalized accordingly.

A home can be minimalistic with only essential items in the home. It is typically designed with relaxing clean lines and plenty of integrated storage to ensure minimal clutter.

A maximalist home includes essentials as well as selective items on display. It is cleverly filled with colors, patterns and shapes for an intriguing and eye-catching effect.

A family home is an eclectic mixture of age adapted items fitted to the growing lifestyle of its family members; it is a busy space of interaction. Regular spring cleaning is required in such households.

A refined home should be aesthetically beautiful, practical to live in and adapted to its occupants.

16/ BE WELL ORGANISED

Organization practicality,
Things are laid impeccably,
The setup is space saving,
Saved time in finding,

Life becomes easier,
No chaos or clutter,
The streamlined life,
Well worth the strife,

Storage optimizing,
Ease access allowing,
Tidy stuff in place,
Maximize the space,

An organized property,
A built-in harmony.

The home ergonomic layout is made to befit the lifestyle of its residents.

A desk or workspace has the right stationery and equipment, paper and documents in folders or filing storage, adequate lighting, comfortable seating and a work inducing environment.

A harmonious person has a well-managed agenda dedicating relevant time for home, work, spouse, family, friends, social outings, health, fitness, self-care, spirituality, self-growth and recreation.

An organized society has the right leaders and infrastructure to cater for the care, development, growth and wellbeing of its community.

17/ BE PRODUCTIVE

Productivity is about getting things done.

Time and work efficiency bring results.

Knowing your learning method and most productive time is key in developing time efficiency.

Obviously, productivity might depend on each person in terms of learning speed and working rhythm. The traditional model of 9-5 working hours is one model for handling tasks.

Do you invest in self-education?

Do you upskill in profession?

Do you nurture personal growing?

Do you optimize when working?

Do you level up your efficiency?

Do you simplify with technology?

Do you complete tasks timely?

Do you delegate practically?

18/ BE MINDFUL OF YOUR TIME

Time is a precious commodity.

Valuing each other's time matters when it is related to dating, social, business appointments and events.

There can be reasons for purposeful lateness, either occasionally or when onn a tight schedule (for extremely busy and important people).

To attend on time is human courtesy and it shows mutual appreciation for our valuable schedule.

To inform prior to lateness and non-attendance is established good behavior.

It is understandable that there can be exceptional occurrences.

Knowing when to excuse oneself whilst invited as a guest is also good etiquette.

We do not overstay as a guest, and we thank the host for their dedicated time and efforts.

Scheduling time is an element of productivity when intense focus is applied.

Time management is essential when multitasking or when managing multiple responsibilities.

Blocking time slots can be a good method for intense, focused work.

Productive time is not measured in length but in efficiency while handling tasks. A short burst of focused activity is better than long hours of desk sitting to get a task done.

An awakened mind, the ability to learn, adaptability, communication and business skills, professional expertise and focused attention are great indicators of work efficiency.

Time management is the productive handling of the 24-hour cycle daily and some of the techniques include:

-The Pomodoro Technique: 25 min time chunks for focused work and 5 minutes rest.

-The 80/20 Pareto Principle: 20% of your efforts dedicated to 80% of the work.

-Eat that frog: do the hardest and most important task first thing in the morning.

-Get Things Done or To-do list: write the list of things that need to be done, prioritize them and get them done.

Time is funny,

Likewise eternity,

Seems never ending,

Death comes knocking,

                                              Birth comes strikingly,

                                              Life is a miracle story,

                                              Nurture every moment,

                                              Delight in the present,

Experimental senses,

Sensory illusion lenses,

                                              Earth is only a fraction,

                                              Galaxies' count a billion,

You think it is reality,

Way beyond what you see,

Your awareness knows best,

The multidimensional crest.

19/ DEVELOP SELF-DISCIPLINE

Self-discipline rigorous,
A strong mindset obvious,

Show up and do, reluctant or loving,
Could be smarter, learn to love doing,

Fulfill your work regularly,
Use willpower productively,

Constancy & responsibility,
Achieve goals intelligently,

First work on all mindsets,
Set goals, do what it takes,

Frequency meets cumulation,
Accrued results to completion,

This society is instant gratification,
Pop-ups & constant distractions,

                                          The grinding is challenging,
                                          Iron mindset for advancing.

Work and persistence,
A wonderful resonance.

Self-discipline is about waking up even when you want to stay in bed, going to work regardless of how you feel, fulfilling your responsibilities without excuse, doing the work that needs to be done, etc.

Good habits are repeated action,
Strength, exercise, musculation,

                                            Restful sleep & recharging,
                                            Good diet for wellbeing,

Step by step compilation,
Make compound addition,

                                          The learned mind is growing,
                                          The trained body following,

Work becomes expertise,
Persistence brings ease,

                                            Frequency feeds credits,
                                            A model life with habits.

20/ AIM FOR COMPLETION

Practice completion.

The brain is wired for goal completion as it triggers you when there are pending tasks. It also affects mind clarity and concentration.

When you start an activity, aim to finish it. Finishing what you start is mindset building. It creates a sense of accomplishment and a feel-good factor.

Celebrating goal achievements increases confidence and it can initiate a thread of serial success.

Thinking about unfinished or endless projects to finalize clutters the brain, so an alternative is to transfer thoughts and write a to-do list.

Being methodical in your approach to tasks means that you follow a process to completion. One simple method is to identify the task, the required resources, the best method to achieve it, the way to simplify it or delegate it and the timeline.

Completion also applies to other aspects of life, such as self-love, healing, managing emotions, handling relationships, etc.

21/ BE SAVVY

A mind of understanding,
Experience true living,

Contemplate the creation,
Behave in conscious motion,

Life experience is teaching,
Discover your inner being,

Draw on logical reasoning,
Sharpen decision making,

Be selective in thinking,
Process emotional feeling,

Manage flow distraction,
Focus, selective action,

Work smart with excellence,
Expert learning to advance,

        Emulate with due diligence,
        Resilience, success sequence,

                Failures mean learning,
                Step by step achieving,

        Cheer yourself constantly,
        Become your best ally,

Inner self master code,
Enhance yourself mode,

        Self-realization in present,
        Eternal bliss magnificent.

22/ SEEK KNOWLEDGE

Learning never stops,
Lessons of life plots,

Dive in full motion
In knowledge ocean,

Unravel to the source,
Raving endless course,

Information overload,
Select your download,

Technology advancement,
Filter what is relevant,

Distractions pop in & snap,
Decide what's right to grasp,

Good knowledge acquisition,

Human growth expansion,

Feed your mind righteously,

For constructive eternity.

Knowledge is an expansive model that spreads into various categories: linguistics, semantics, syntax, vocabulary, grammar, rhetoric, scientific data, data acquisition, data analysis, interpretation, sensorial learning, practical experimentation, reflection, logical reasoning, problem solving, epistemology, etc.

Sensorial knowledge is acquired by our five senses. We perceive information visually, auditory, olfactory, kinesthetically and physically.

Intrinsic knowledge is linked to intuition, inner knowing, gut feeling, transcendental knowledge, inspiration, etc.

The mental grasp of knowledge is based on subjective experience and personal references, whether conscious or subconscious.

The infancy of knowledge starts with the learning process and attempts to unravel comprehension.

Proficiency is acknowledged with the practice of its teachings.

Knowledge is mastered when understood, applied and taught.

Human life is a learning curve and an experimental journey.

Education is sought to grow and perfect oneself. When will, work and dedication accompany data acquisition and analysis, skills are learnt.

The human mind is built for knowledge management, while the soul thrives on growth and expansion.

23/ GROW MINDSET CLARITY

Mind clarity is about conscious thinking, meaning that you pay attention to what goes on in your brain.

Selecting your thoughts is a transformative skill that requires cultivating awareness to recondition the mindset.

Declutter the space from mindless thoughts and negative prompts to initiate the right thought process.

Select and prioritize what matters to you and work accordingly.

Your life experience and conditioning might have created some thoughts and behaviors that you may want to revisit and transform into fruitful thoughts.

Unlearning and relearning are essential for mind reset.

There are plenty of existing techniques for awareness and mindset building.

In auto-pilot mode, we routinely follow a set of habits and flicker between past and prospective thoughts.

Disrupt the thought process,

To enter mindfulness,

Be focused and present,
Eternity is omniscient,

                                      Awakened mind perceiving,
                                      Self-fulfilling and satisfying,

Sensorial reality made attractive,
Timeless joyful moments to live,

                                      Life miracle is blissful,
                                      Blessed enlightened soul.

24/ SHOW PROFESSIONALISM

Model professionalism,
Behavior perfectionism,

A charismatic stance,
Reverential excellence,

Leading respectful conduct,
Business acumen construct,

Competency & reliability,
Soft skills & sociability,

Refined speech presentation,
Fluent in artful persuasion,

Professionalism is learnable,

For those willing and able,

> *Learning and upskilling,*
> *For business improving,*

A deftly skilled combination,
Great demeanor inspiration,

> *Personal and business etiquette,*
> *Benchmark in mastery skillset,*

Know-how to handle artfully,
People & contexts intelligently,

> *Poised professional fluent,*
> *Field of expertise eloquent,*

Drive business consciously,
For a constructive society,

Model work inspiration,

Masterpiece achievement.

25/ KNOW RESPECT

Self-respect triggers respect.

When you show consideration to yourself and others, it is reciprocated.

Self-respect is about valuing who you are as a spiritual being having a human experience.

It is self-acceptance and owning your own values and principles.

It encompasses knowing your worth, standing up for yourself, learning how to say no, setting boundaries, possessing a growth mindset, managing emotions, doing the right thing, relaxing your mind and being yourself.

Self-dignity implies taking care of yourself, your environment and your inner world.

> **Bible, Exodus 20:12** "Honor your father and your mother, that your days may be long in the land that the Lord your God is giving you."

Bible, Matthew 7:12 "So whatever you wish that others would do to you, do also to them, for this is the Law and the Prophets."

Bible, 1 Peter 2.17 Show proper respect to everyone, love the family of believers, fear God, honor the emperor.

26/ CULTIVATE THE RIGHT CULTURE

There is a culture that breeds from your ethnicity. It often relates to food choice, ethnic clothing, music, original language, country of origin, ancestors' cult, etc.

Your ethnic cultural heritage is something that you may wish to cultivate and pass on to your lineage.

There is a society culture that we all contribute to influence, and this is the one we need to ponder upon.

A simplified caricature of the current society would illustrate how human behavior has been affected by the tech-based lifestyle (being online and always available), enhanced body image (filters, cosmetic surgery, beauty adds-on), sexualized online portals (only fans role models), gender blur, women objectification, promiscuous mentality, hook up culture, primal animalistic behavior, dumbing entertainment, etc. This culture is rewarding nudity and sex.

What type of society are we creating?

What is the better alternative?

Value based culture, solid principles, noble character building, healthy lifestyle, positive mindset, finding your human purpose, family building, community focus, forward and evolved thinking, having lofty goals, building a constructive society and legacy, inspiring role models, etc.

What about swapping things around and making the real things valuable such as loyalty, morals, noble character, principles, values, etc.?

That move would elevate human consciousness.

27/ BE A GOOD ROLE MODEL

What lofty goals have you in mind?
What legacy will you mastermind?
What impact in this world round?
What will create your echo sound?
What miracle will you design?
What is in it for mankind?

Are we getting wiser?
Are we making it better?
Are we world destroyers?
Are we society builders?
Are our civilizations greater?
Are our kingdoms superior?

THE MASCULINE

Strong muscles, body bravery,
Protective, armor responsibility,

Leading manager visionary,
Enriched provider mentality,

Sane and mature gentleman,
With morals and ethical plan,

A considerate man of his word,
Driven, focused, leader of the herd,

Resourceful and problem solver,
Well-spoken and smart educator,

Planner, manager, skilled master,
Team builder, collaborative helper,

Honorable respected authority,
Pragmatic thinker, predatory,

A chivalrous, courteous charmer,
Confident, ambitious, initiative taker,

Gifted communicator with charisma,
Spiritually endowed, wise enigma,

Fun sparks' outbursts with family,
Sociable, environmentally friendly,

Upheld dangerous and competitive,
Fearful character when imperative,

Loyal to values and family,
Attractive and fit naturally,

Earnest, conscious, grounded human,

Awakened to God-man spiritual plan.

THE FEMININE

The pretty poise of beauty,
Elegance and femininity,

Attractiveness in play mode,
Sophisticated seduction code,

The art of female sensuality,
In the curve designed body,

The layers of goddess mystery,
A higher realm of spirituality,

The epitome of heartful passion,
The instinctive gut of intuition,

In womb and maternal bonding,
Raising, rearing and nurturing,

The wide range of expression,
Female model communication,

Smart, clever and well-mannered,
Dignified with a noble character,

Holding self-respect in her living,
Self-assured, strong and enduring,

Powerful, resilient and forgiving,
Compassionate, empathetic, loving,

Genuinely authentic and giving,
Fragile, delicate and caring,

Skillfully diplomatic and adaptable,
Spiritual, optimistic and reliable,

Fun-excited, joyful, enjoyable,
Patient, helpful, adaptable,

Vulnerable in a safe environment,
Stylishly respectful and confident,

Faithful in emotional feeling,
Self-care routine for well-being,

Wild in erratic behavior,
Calm in delicate demeanor,

Endowed with motherhood instinct,
Complex feminine, an intense link.

THE EARTH PENDULUM

Masculine and feminine energy,
Balanced beings in harmony,

The Yin and Yang equilibrium,
Strong genders in the continuum,

Excess unbalance in androgyny breeds,
Endangered survival of human species,

Tech advancement, AI evolution,
Trend uniformity standardization,

Autoreply bots communicate,
Acronym smiley chat literate,

Personalized human touch,
The multidimensional rush,

Evil and good deeds inclination,

Destroy and build interaction,

Wickedness or sacred influencing,

Darkening faces or enlightening.

28/ BE RESPONSIBLE

While it might sound like common sense, taking responsibility is an integral part of becoming an adult.

We take responsibility for our thoughts, actions and behavior and for whatever is incumbent upon us.

To be entrusted with a mind, heart, body and soul means that all aspects of the being need to be catered for in our human experience.

It starts from the self - inside and out - and in the familial, social and societal environment.

To be responsible means to fulfil your human role at home, at work and in society as a whole.

When we are responsible, we self-construct, we do not play the victim, we do not blame, we avoid self-pity, we fall and rise again, we develop skills, we grow, we empower ourselves and others to do what is required.

We become conscious, dutiful, timely, accountable, pragmatic, aware, productive, dedicated, self-disciplined and goal orientated.

We rise to the challenge of life as action-takers.

Each sane adult has a level of responsibility in the family unit, the community and in humanity.

29/ BE PRESENTABLE

Fashion has evolved in history,
Hats, gloves and gowns beauty,

Exquisite dress, fluffy & flowy,
Sophistication & must accessory,

Smart tailored suit & hankie,
Skillful grooming, elegantly,

Modern times, wicky & twisty,
Ripped jeans & leggings flexi,

T-shirts and crop tops, flashy,
Track suits & trainers manly,

Urban dress code is gender free,
A flesh show time of diversity,

                        Comfortable clothes movement,
                        No need for classy arrangement,

                        Cool and streetwear uptrend,
                        Cap, hoodie and swear blend,

                        Changing styles in fashion trend,
                        Your personal preference brand,

Freedom of choice in dressing,
What image are you embodying?

Whatever you decide to wear,
Reflects your chosen character.

An array of fabric and texture,

A crafted palette in fashion color.

Fashion is inclusive.

Clothing is often linked to fashion trends, culture, religion, dress code, business attire, location, weather, convenience, body type, practicality, protocol, social rank, uniform, taste, personal preference, character, finance and the value you attach to it.

Being presentable is about looking good, clean and groomed.

Dressing well often increases wellbeing and confidence.

Branded clothes or not, quality and fit are essential.

30/ BE AGREEABLE

Is being nice a weakness?
Grand gesture of kindness,

Signal character affability,
Openminded agreeability,

A mind in receptive mode,
Sympathetic human abode,

Diligent, reliable, trustful,
Smart, assertive, helpful,

Sharing good countenance,
With a centered confidence,

Your good side is showing,
For relationship nurturing,

A multifaceted magnet,
Grumpy, happy, upset,

Sad, angry or loving,
Affability is inviting,

Diplomatic, approachable,
Appreciative and sociable,

Cultivating a grateful mindset,
A strong presence fills the set,

Skilled in managing emotion,
Countenance in commotion,

Showing love beautifully,
To close ones and family,

A smile in face friendly,
Respond courteously,

Greeting and politeness,
A helping hand in progress,

Affability in the demeanor,
A trait of noble character.

31/ PRACTICE SELF CONTROL

Self-control is mastery,
Acquire this great ability,
Monitor the thought entry,
Craft actions precisely,

Observe emotions flowing,
The cognitive processing,
Pre-fontal cortex mining,
The brain is self-regulating,

Manage neural connection,
Skillful communication,
Master your own decision,
Strong willed interaction,

Self-restraint is empowering,
Loosening in good timing,

At mind games excelling,

The intelligence of being.

> **Bible, Proverbs 25.28** A man without self-control is like a city broken into and left without walls.
>
> **Bible, Galatians 5.22-23** But the fruit of the Spirit is love, joy, peace, patience, kindness, goodness, faithfulness, gentleness, self-control; against such things there is no law.

The animalistic behavior,

An instinctive feral vigor,

An energy scattering core.

The mindset of a rational,

Calculating, transactional,

In control of the primal.

The lofty behavior rule,

Blessed, selective, fruitful,

Focused, deliberate, cup full.

32/ SHARPEN YOUR SAW

Ensure that you stay sharp.

Renew and develop yourself when it is time to do so.

Sharpening your saw relates to constant self-awareness and acquiring new skills set when relevant.

Your best asset is yourself.

Look after your multidimensional self that needs to be cared for, developed and looked after so it grows fit for purpose.

Take time to disconnect and recharge the human battery.

Learn to nurture and develop all aspects of yourself.

Be clever and work smart, not hard.

> **Bible, Ecclesiastes 10.10** If the axe is dull and he does not sharpen its edge, then he must exert more strength. Wisdom has the advantage of giving success.
>
> **Bible, Exodus, 20.8-10** Six days you shall labor and do all your work, but the seventh day is the Sabbath of the Lord your God. In it you shall do no work

33/ DEVELOP CHARISMA

Charisma is an energy blueprint.

Charisma embodies an exceptional character, a noticeable presence, a remarkable beauty, eye catching looks, a confident spirit, a perfectly groomed individual, a tastefully stylish person, a highly attractive specimen, exceptional skills, impressive abilities, a compelling influence, a powerful leader, an inspirational figure, etc.

Fox Cabane identifies four categories of charisma: focused (attentive listening towards others like Oprah), visionary (inspiring vision like Elon Musk), kindness (warmth and emotional intelligence like spiritual leaders) and authority (power and social status with elites).

I would add a spiritual category for divinely anointed guides (prophets and messengers).

Charisma is a magnetic energy that attracts.

Aristotle associates it with the combined chemistry of logos (reasoned rhetoric), ethos (character credibility) and pathos (arousing emotions).

A charismatic person is noticeable. The room senses the energy switch once in presence.

Charisma is expressed with powerful communication, recognizable traits and character with the effect of causing an emotional impact.

Charisma is energy,

A source intensity,

Hypnotic tension,

Heartfelt emotion,

Vibrating presence,

Inner knowing sense,

A touch of mystery,

Magnetic mastery,

In words & beyond,

Vibrating God bond,

A significant mark,

Earth living spark.

34/ KNOW THYSELF

'Know thyself' is an ancient Greep aphorism at the entrance of Apollo temple. It directs to an introspective assessment of the self.

The conscious and rational part of the mind manages the understanding of the self and its place in the world.

The internal quest is the search for answers to philosophical questions such as who we are and what is the purpose of our existence. This leads to pondering on the multidimensional reality and the existence of the soul.

For Socrates, it is knowing what you know and what you do not know while acknowledging the immortality of the soul.

Plato's allegory of the cave concept implies an esoteric knowledge to be discovered to free yourself and unveil genuine knowledge.

According to empiricist David Hume, it is about understanding how our past experiences, perceptions and emotions have shaped our habits and way of life.

While Immanuel Kant assumes that all humans experience a similar structure of reality, post-Kant philosophers assume that each individual constructs a subjective notion of the human realm.

The proactive Friedrich Nietzsche advocates the unique perspective of the individual to become empowered and to create a life that is befitting.

The existentialist Sartre promotes the free will to define your own life and your prospective future.

The postmodern philosophical interpretation explains how your identity has often been shaped by ethnic, socio-cultural, geographical, religious and political factors.

Knowing Thyself is the act of introspection to become aware of the inner self.

Knowing Thyself in spirituality is the mystic approach to the inner dimension and the divine energy.

35/ LIVE THE PRESENT

'Carpe Diem' in Latin embodies the spirit of living the moment.

Living in the now relates to being present and aware. It sounds logical and yet, we are wired to experience a constant stream of thoughts often geared to past and future. Thus, it is only with a conscious mind that one can become aware of the present moment.

Now is the only reality,

The past is a log memory.

The future is anticipation.

The present is realization.

The Now feeds liveliness,

Live creation blissfulness.

Fully exalt the moment,

Thus, become present,

Heart and mind energy,
Body and soul synergy,

Past and future dispelled,
Now thought bedazzled,

Focus on the breathing,
Body movements rising,

Sense the environment,
A sensory amazement,

Live pleasure awareness,
Radiating consciousness,

Mechanical mode bygone,
Mindfulness switch is on,

Magical beauty of creation,

Awakened human passion,

       Exchanges are profound,

       Senses feel surround,

              Emotions are shared,

              Love belongs there.

Mindfulness is to quieten the mind and silently perceive the sensorial reality.

It is hearing the body talk, the heart speech, the soul wonder and the mind in awe of the sensorial expression.

Mindfulness brings relief and soothes.

A mindful moment is perfect.

It is eternity in motion.

Living in the now is to enjoy the experience of life.

While you have goals and objectives, appreciate the journey that takes you there.

The starting point, the trip and the destination are all part of the package.

This is why happiness starts from where you are.

Happiness has no conditions.

"I will be happy when..."

If you are not happy now, it is unlikely that you will ever be.

Happiness is a mindset that breeds from gratitude and contentment.

As you become appreciative, your wellbeing grows.

As your wellbeing grows, you focus more on the positive.

As you do so, you attract better and become happier.

36/ CHANGE YOURSELF FIRST

Change starts from within.

We often notice what is wrong in others instead of looking within ourselves.

The first step is to look in your own backyard and see what needs to be done.

Fix yourself before trying to fix others.

> **Bible, Matthew 7.3** "Why do you look at the speck of sawdust in your brother's eye and pay no attention to the plank in your own eye?

When you are focused on self-improvement, you do not have time to go around for small talk, gossiping, backbiting and spotting others' flaws. Instead, you direct your energy on constructive mindset development.

Changing yourself is holding yourself accountable for your results and working towards becoming the best version of you.

Are you monitoring your thoughts?

Are you dispelling negative thoughts?

Do you reform unhealthy habits?

Do you transform questionable traits?

Do you remove yourself from toxic environments?

Do you take the steps towards self-reform?

37/ BE FORGIVING

Forgiveness starts with yourself.

Making mistakes is an essential part of being human and often failures are the best teaching lessons.

Taking accountability of your perfect imperfection and continuing to learn are signs that you are making progress.

Learning to stand up after a fall makes striving worthwhile.

Self-forgiveness is self-care.

Dwelling on past mistakes and holding grudges spread negative energy.

What is depression?

Pain obliteration,

Feel the emptiness,

Step in carelessness,

Fuel for addiction,

Forget time motion,

Fumes inhaling,
Excess dwelling,

Spiral annihilation,
To evade illusion,

Emotions crushing,
Heart convoluting,

Accept the passing,
Hurt & pain feeling,

Build the resolve,
Move on & evolve.

Next step in action,
Positive activation,

Nurture your being,
Nourish wellbeing,

Move in your body,
Sports flexibility,

                Landscape strolling,
                    Forest reviving,

                                  Sea & sand motion,
                                    Enthralling horizon,

                Outdoors healing,
                Magic beginning,

Self-care grooming,
New hair styling,
                Pamper and revive,
                An activity to thrive,

                                  Enjoy superfoods,

Reset the moods,

The body temple,
Fresh reassemble,

Loved ones linking,
Mingling rekindling,

Healing the wounds,
In spa lagoons,

Resurrect your joy,
Revive heart enjoy,

Woken perception,
Enliven projection,

Mesmerizing skies,
Bewilder the eyes,

Cosmic vibration,
Heart link cohesion,

Sigh turn to smiling,
Mind rekindle loving,

Soul wonder wander,
Marvel bliss thunder,

Now is the moment,
Enchanting present,

Miraculous living,
Sparkle bewitching,

Mystic spirit delight,
Supernatural light.

Reflect on past experiences and what they are meant to teach you.

Love yourself enough to forgive your imperfections and acts of foolishness.

Forgiveness to oneself is self-love.

Forgiveness to others purifies the heart.

Being forgiving is the simple acceptance of human flaws.

The soothing act of forgiveness has a warm healing effect.

It is an act of love.

>**Bible, Luke 6.37** "Do not judge, and you will not be judged. Do not condemn, and you will not be condemned. Forgive, and you will be forgiven."

>**Bible, Ephesians 4.31** "Get rid of all bitterness, rage and anger, brawling and slander, along with every form of malice."

>**Quran, 42.43** "And whoever is patient and forgives- indeed, that is of the matters worthy of resolve."

38/ BE AUTHENTIC

Authenticity is truthfulness.

How is authenticity linked to evil and good?

There is a feel-good factor after any good deed that is done (such as a smile, a gift, a donation, giving help, collective working or a humanitarian act).

This reinforces the idea that constructive goodness is the preferred human behavior for our species evolution, simply because the opposite (evil spread) would lead to human self-destruction.

Being authentic is to become your true self, on the scriptural basis that human nature is intrinsically inclined towards beneficence and benevolence.

> **Bible Philippians 4.8** "Finally, brothers, whatever is true, whatever is honorable, whatever is just, whatever is pure, whatever is lovely, whatever is commendable, if there is any excellence, if there is anything worthy of praise, think about these things."
>
> **Bible 2 Timothy 3.16-17** "All Scripture is breathed out by God and profitable for teaching, for reproof, for correction, and for training in righteousness, that the

man of God may be complete, equipped for every good work."

Heart, mind, body and soul are aligned to your purpose.

Authenticity creates energy vibrations attuned to the whole being.

Authenticity is rawness in thought and action.

When in the flow, tailored speech and actions follow.

Genuineness in character is sincerity.

Authentic emotions are connected to heart-centeredness.

39/ BE LOVING

Love is spirited vitality,
Mountain collapse instantly,

Knowing love is epitome,
Birth of life extraordinary,

Love electrifies moments,
Love stirs up sentiments,

Love smiles at daydreamers,
Love sustains crave lovers,

Love is beauty inspiring,
Endless source of being,
Amazing way of living,

Passion enthralling,

Sensory arousing,
Lit sparks fusing,

                                          Minds amazement,
                                          Bodies entanglement,
                                          Emotion commitment,

Live bodies melting,
Warm hearts sharing,
Stirred minds smiling,

                                          Excited animation,
                                          Curious expansion,
                                              Soul elevation,

True love is quenching,
Incredibly satisfying,
Invariably boldening.

Loving heart radiance,
Twinkling body dance,
Mind fired up intense,
Raised spirit trance,

Love adorns all existence.
Fill deep heart expanse.
Live body cells sense,
Intimate deep romance,

Seduced exploration,
Mysterious adulation,
Excitement adoration,
Soul esoteric devotion,

Divine grace union,
Miraculous passion,
Love bond connection,
Infinity communion.

The heart source is abundant and boundless.

> **Bible, Corinthians 13.4-7** Love is patient, love is kind. It does not envy, it does not boast, it is not proud. It does not dishonor others, it is not self-seeking, it is not easily angered, it keeps no record of wrongs. Love does not delight in evil but rejoices with the truth. It always protects, always trusts, always hopes, always perseveres.
>
> **Bible, 1 Corinthians 16:14** Let all that you do be done in love.
>
> **Bible, John 13:34-35** "I am giving you a new commandment, that you love one another. Just as I have loved you, so you too are to love one another. By this, everyone will know that you are My disciples if you have love and unselfish concern for one another."

Self-love is wellbeing,

Mastering art healing,

Healthy mind foundation,
Relationship realization,

                                Self-aware and assertive,
                                Balanced and proactive,

You value your wellness,
Body soul sharpness,

                                Mind heart symbiosis,
                                Self-reform analysis,

Love yourself in bits,
Develop good habits,

                                When growth exhibits,
                                Your best self-hits.

******

Great love unconditional,
Such a boundless miracle,

                                      A constant cup pouring,
                                      A source never ending,

Longest winding river,
Overpowering shiver,

                                      Eternal fountain flow,
                                      Christ gleaming glow,

Expand enlightening,
Love illuminating.

                                      Beyond soul shiver,
                                      Love eternal river.

40/ BE NON-JUDGEMENTAL

First impressions always integrate some type of judgment, prejudice or categorization, based on what is familiar and known in our life experience.

Our perception of the world is subjective, so the inner world engrains how we see people and the world.

We typically judge people on how they look, dress, speak, do, behave and the beliefs/values they stand for.

It is an innate social behavior.

To become more open minded and accepting, we need to see beyond appearances and reflect on the divine dimension within.

Disrupted by certain traits?

Which energy vibe imprints?

Are we alike? Self-projecting?

Are we meant to learn something?

Inner work mirroring?

Are we really judging?

Others or self-reflection?
Switch back into action,

Read the reverberation,
Make self-transformation,

Embed a revised perception,
Positive thought impression,

Transform your inner world,
Constructive creation mold.

If the world is a subjective perception, then our inner world is reflected outwardly. If we want the world to be non-judgmental, we must start with ourselves and become non-judgmental.

41/ BE VULNERABLE

To be vulnerable is to be open and show your true self in the right context.

In self-care, vulnerability equates to shadow work and healing the inner parts of yourself.

In social relationships, vulnerability breeds relatability and trust.

In love, it creates authentic bonding and intimacy.

Being vulnerable means facing uncertainty, fear, rejection, risk and emotional exposure.

Conscious vulnerability is choosing to express yourself, talk about your feelings, share a personal story, ask for help, make that call, accept yourself in all your perfect greatness and weakness.

Being vulnerable is learning to trust again after past betrayal, loving again after heartaches, showing up after failures, entering a relationship after healing yourself, admitting your flaws and mistakes, apologizing, forgiving, etc.

Deciding to face the challenge of vulnerability is brave.

Knowing vulnerability,

A show of sensibility,

All those built-in walls,

Protective strong holds,

Not showing weakness,

The fear of helplessness,

The heart being exposed,

The mind worries caused,

The trust at open hands,

The loving bond blends,

The possible heartache,

Can I make a mistake?

                      Perfect imperfectness,

                      Yes, not being flawless,

Stand up after falling,

Pick up pieces aching,

Learning forgiveness,

For others & oneself,

Healing completely,

Soul, mind & body,

           Show up mine terrain,

           Rise up again & again,

Growth mindset resolve,

Learn to problem solve.

42/ BE ASSERTIVE

Assertiveness is confidence,
Wrists on the table stance,

A confident personality,
Know thy self clearly,

Thy worth a known fix,
'Bring it on' in the mix,

Assertiveness is acceptance,
Born from self-confidence,

Master art and ability,
Not an approval needy,

Communication is key,
Know yourself rightly,

Ask your wants clearly,

Fix your boundary,

Speech eloquence,

Emotion sense,

Constructed mindset,

Idea, thought reset,

Effective communication,

Confidence evolution.

Confidence is distinct from ego, arrogance, aggressiveness and bullying. It is rather self-empowerment, acceptance and acknowledgment of your whole being.

Confidence is to believe in yourself, your potential, your goals and your ability to achieve success.

43/ PLAN AND PREPARE

Preparation is the most crucial step prior to execution.

Planning is anticipation and preparation review for your endeavor.

When you plan, you are better equipped to achieve realization.

Thinking ahead means fast forwarding the steps to get the result.

Preparation effectively saves time in the long run.

Mental rehearsal includes mindset building, skillset review, prepping the action, understanding the why, getting the motivation, clarifying the goals, learning, training, applying knowledge, staying focused, envisioning the result, etc .

Physical preparation is training the body.

Emotional preparation is self-love and healing.

Preparation is the stepping stone for deliberate action.

Planning is preparation,

Anticipate expectation,

Foresee the unexpected,

Knowing the upcoming,

Acquire field mastery,
Professional virtuosity,
Constant in progress,
Persistent in process,

Upskilling & adapting,
And visionary trending,
Think, imagine creation,
Spontaneous inspiration,

Bold and deliberate,
Ready to checkmate,
Hurdles tamper the way,
Jump, kick, find a way,

The readiness for challenge,
Failure and success branch,
Always ready whenever,
Strive and win endeavor.

44/ BE BOLD

                                              Be brave like David,

                                              And grow the star seed,

Stand up for yourself,

As a unique self,

                                              Show up every day,

                                              Be responsive today,

Awaken & tone up,

Drink water, rise up,

Be clean & groomed,

Dress up all bloomed,

Become a shining ray,

Feel alive each day,

Acknowledge who you are,

A divine soul, work of art,

The masterpiece higher being,

Grand revelation incoming,

Answer the call of becoming,

'I am what I am' in being,

The sheer perplexity 'I am,'

In its immense anagram,

Mind blowing awareness,

The Divine Consciousness.

45/ BECOME FIT

Fitness is a source of wellbeing.

Physical strength affects your energy levels.

In a sedentary lifestyle, it is a prerequisite to practice some type of physical activity to maintain a level of fitness.

There is so much choice in sports depending on whether one wishes to build strength, endurance, cardio, stretching and/or balance. Even speed walking is a great cardiovascular activity that oxygenizes the body.

Sport is a major source of wellbeing. As you become fitter, you are more dynamic and better at mood and stress management. Mental faculties improve with exercise and there is a lower risk of chronic diseases.

Outdoor activities are a wonderful way to revitalize and recharge the mind, body and spirit. Feeling the connection with nature and the universe is soul awakening. Breathing the purified air in green flowery zones and arboraceous parks is greatly rejuvenating. When living in urban cities, walking in landscaped gardens is inspiringly beautiful and refreshing.

With regular practice, the variety and amount of physical activity can be gradually increased to achieve the required level of fitness.

Athletes, fitness role models and sports coaches are splendid examples in highlighting the benefits of fitness training. Many of the top influencers have inspired young men to become physically fit.

Puffy, fluffy, muscular,
Strong, brave, runner,
Mind conditioning,
Body fit training,

Superfood nutrition,
Workout selection,
Sport and discipline,
Wellness tracking,

Energy stamina,
Mindfulness aura,
Spirited mindset,
Body soul reset,

Thought shaping,
Enhanced wellbeing,
Supreme vitality,
Echoing vibrancy,

Consciously steering,
Extraordinary being,
Seeds of greatness,
As God & goddess.

46/ EAT WELL

It is worth noticing how nature has provided such a variety of food in hues of color, texture and taste.

Listen to your body to know what food fits best.

Whatever your diet, there is an enormous selection that complements your daily food intake.

Believers have access to Kosher, Halal and religiously symbolic food.

Vegan, Vegetarian, flexitarian and meat eaters have a global food supply chain.

Dieters have the option to follow any trending or chosen diet.

Organic food is found everywhere and if required, food can also be grown in your own garden or allotment.

Worldwide ingredients and dishes can now be experienced for the heightened pleasure of our delighted taste buds.

The saying "We are what we eat" is a great incentive for conscious eating.

Homemade food, prepared with love and good intention, and eaten mindfully, provides a full nourishment. Food can fulfill hunger or become a sensorial experience.

The food experience can translate into a sophisticated dinner, tasty and colorful dishes, artful table decoration, and family/social gatherings to create and share memorable moments.

It is worth being mindful when eating.

The cuisine of savoring,

An experimental living,

Munching on a brunch,

Masticating with crunch,

Spice awakening mouth,

Flavorsome North South,

Textures unwrapping,

Taste buds vibrating,

Food morsels in dips,

Delicious fingertips,

Cutlery, shop stick,

Clay, metallic click,

Earthenware, bamboo,
Porcelain plate preview,
Napkin ring in place,
Ready, set the pace,

Appetizing starter,
Sneaky taste flavor,
Main mighty meat,
Saucy sauce feast,

Side dish accompany,
Carbohydrates fiery,
Veggies brush color,
Belly blush sensor,

Hard, soft, squishy,
Fruit, salad, pastry,
Yoghurt melting pot,

Nuts mix, seeds lot,

Tart, pie, cake run,
Butter bread, hot bun,
Dessert in flamboyant,
Tantalizing complement,

Baklava love layering,
Ice cream tub licking,
Post-dinner greets tea,
Chocolates meet coffee,

Sparkles bubble water,
Infused drinks wonder,
Citrus ginger tickles,
Cinnamon mint riddles,

Radiant eyes jubilate,
Energy grow celestial,
Heart peak ebullient,

Echoing luminescent,

Sweeten lips hydrate,
Velvet skin delectate,
Edible delicacy,
Ecstatic sensory.

47/ HYDRATE YOURSELF

Drinking water is essential for hydration.

Planet Earth is composed of around 70% water.

There is an average of 60% water in the human body and 90% water in the blood.

Water is the best hydration drink.

Aim for at least 8 to 10 glasses of water per day, best complemented with whole food elements.

There are other known hydrating liquids such as coconut water, electrolyte drinks, milk and dairy alternative, fruit infused water, caffeine free teas, etc.

The most hydrating veggies are watermelon and cucumber.

Fruit and vegetable smoothies are ideal for quenching thirst and absorbing vitamins at the same time.

When you are thirsty, you are already dehydrated. Urine color is a good thirst indicator; the lighter the color, the more hydrated you are.

Hot drinks like caffeinated coffee can dehydrate; this is why water hydration is necessary.

Take sips of aliveness,
Breathe in divine bless,

Aqua trickle flow,
Winding river show,
Blend in deep sea,
Wild ocean roar free,

High waves are foaming,
Slashing and slamming,
Rocks draw a part,
Sand scrambles art,

Cliffs cultivate erosion,
Caves & ponds creation,
Mountains move along,
Ice glaciers stay strong,

Fluff white snow woolen,

Chilled ice cubes soften,
Boiling thermal spring,
Hot drink warming,

The zigzagging currents,
Make rhythmic moments,
Echolocation zooming,
Vibrational rolling,

Hues of blues horizon,
Green algae in season,
Tidal waves warming,
Crisp water cooling,

Fresh splash in spills,
Sentient body thrills,
Soaked dermic drench,
Soppy skin say quench,

Fresh water gulp,
Cool throat jump,
Slid liquid run,
Hydration began,

Float or dive in,
Drink, slurp in,
Rub vigorously,
Shower in lively,

Foam, rinse, soak,
Spray, swim, poke,
The aquatic dance,
A synchro sequence,

Flow water energy,
Exalting vitality.

48/ PRACTICE SELF-CARE

How do you look after yourself?

Allocating time to nurture the mind, body and soul is an essential part of self-care. Spending dedicated energy towards your own well-being is fuel recharge.

Do you spend time for self-care?

Doing what makes you feel happy and good, through hobbies, passions, interests, contemplation, nature strolls, holidays, daily care routines, is good for relaxation.

How do you feed your soul?

Breathwork, meditation, prayer and cosmic awareness contribute to soul awakening.

What do you feed your mind?

The mind feeds on knowledge, and the best information to seek is beneficial and constructive.

What do you feed your physical body?

The body is like a vessel that absorbs foods, drinks, oils, creams, perfumes, energies, vibes, etc.

The body clock radio,

Sensory route stereo,

Vibrate transmission,
Open to reception,

What vibes are you in?
In what surroundings?

Feeling deep emotion,
Peak high vibration,
Entering mindfulness,
Wellbeing consciousness,

Feel nature stroking,
Tree leaves bending,
Wind sends salutation,
Sun rays' illumination,

Shrub grass shivering,
Skin dew caressing,
Rain droplets knocking,

Soil screams reviving,

Foot in magnetic ion,

Earth magnetization.

49/ FIND TIME FOR DETOX

Detoxing is healthy.

There are moments for detox, rest and recharge.

Allocate time to switch off and reset mind, body and soul.

For the body, the digestive system can relax with fasting, water/juice fasting, intermittent fasting, diet change, etc.

For the mind, detox might include putting aside technology, emptying your mind, disrupting your thought process, sleeping, enjoying nature, doing nothing, etc.

For the soul, it is about focusing on light and positive energy, meditating, praying, practicing mindfulness, cultivating divine awareness, etc.

For the self, it might be spending time alone to recharge and reset yourself.

Detox is addicting,

A joy in discovering,

Beyond the illusion,

An incredible motion,

Pattern interrupting,
Mind body resetting,
Awaken rejuvenation,
Novel experimentation,

Recharging batteries,
Creating new energies,
Sublimating moment,
Exalting the present,

Mindfulness salutes,
Joyfulness executes,
Eternity hovering,
Divine sublime in.

50/ DO QUALITY TIME

Do and value quality time.

Nowadays, we often sit in the same room with each person busy on their portable device!

Quality time is about being present with your loved ones, doing common activities, communicating to one another, being conscious and acknowledging each other's presence.

Quality time is valuable as it creates those shared moments and cherished memories.

Choosing to be fully present for each human interaction and communication improves connections and relationships.

Quality time creates those incredible and magical moments that make life interesting and memorable.

Life is a worthwhile journey enriched with quality times within the human experience.

Cherish the moment you hold,

Mindful quality time upload,

Who would you rather accompany?

A sound mind, soul and body,

Blessed lives interacting,
Mutual love bonding,
Spirited heart energy,
Blissful soul eternity,

Linked mindsets create,
Partners aim straight,
Passionate junction,
Apex elevation.

51/ FEEL GOOD

When you positively feel good, it impacts your being and lifestyle.

You instinctively change how you treat yourself and how you behave.

You make healthier food choices; you hydrate and exercise.

You take care of yourself and take time to do what is required.

You become focused on self-development and growth.

You are more careful of what goes inside your body.

You know what energies you want to attract.

You know who you want to hang out with.

You make better use of your time.

You are fulfilled from the inside.

You become more conscious.

You choose quality.

You transform.

Grateful and content,

Wholeness enjoyment,

Satisfaction & passion,
Smile in core radiation,

Deep inner fulfillment,
Echoing transcendent,

Heart vortex magnetic,
Vibrations electric,

The happiness essence,
Harmony quintessence,

Soul realm serenity,
Enlightened felicity.

52/ AVOID WASTAGE

To minimize waste is an act of gratefulness.

When we appreciate what we have, we take care of it.

It is easy to get carried away with possessing more and more material things, and a clever way to make sense of things is to identify the purpose of what you own.

Review what you possess and assess everything prior to buying more.

Do you love it?

Do you need it?

Do you utilize it?

Do you enjoy looking at it?

Does it serve a purpose?

Do you take care of it?

Is it relevant in your life?

Is it a cherished item?

Does it bring happy memories?

Does it have sentimental value?

In the case of food that is perishable, is it eatable?

Is the expiry date still valid?

Eating leftovers is a great teaching example.

Regarding technology, is it in working order?

Repairable?

Worth donating?

Owning things that matter, that you love and enjoy, is appreciable and something to be thankful for.

Overbuying and wasting is not a sign of gratefulness.

Obviously, products have a life cycle and upgrading items can be required.

You don't need it,

You don't like it,

You don't want it,

Can you recycle it?
Can you donate it?
Can you repair it?

You love it,
You want it,
You enjoy it,

Are you giving it space?
Are you grateful for it?
Are you caring for it?

53/ INTENTION MATTERS

Actions speak and intentions matter.

Intention creates a value attached action.

An act, endowed with goodness intent, is praiseworthy.

A sincere and heart-felt action is trustworthy.

A well-intended gesture is considerate.

Intentions are transformation catalysts.

The doing is transformed into something greater and more meaningful.

An activity, once dedicated to God, can become an act of worship.

Of course, intentions matter,

What, why, before & after?

What triggers your action?

Impulse, move or decision?

Positive thought structure?

Strategic goal endeavor?

Religious motivation?

Beneficial evolution?

Love and feeling?

Energy bursting?

Philanthropy?

Spirituality?

Soul within?

A win-win?

Conquest?

Success?

54/ ENTER A SACRED UNION

Dating has become an interesting field.

When we enter the dating arena, there are questions to ponder upon.

> *What relationship model do I look for?*
> *What type of connection am I ready for?*

Am I healed substantially?
Do I feel complete already?

> *Am I feeling all right?*
> *Are my priorities right?*

What criteria matter most?
What objectives do I host?

> *What would be most fulfilling?*

Relationship and wellbeing.

Casual relationships are often based on one human dimension (physical chemistry). Long-term commitment is more selective and encompasses the multidimensional being with its compatibility in heart, mind, character, body and soul.

How do you meet your potential partner?

Nowadays, the meeting routes include social media connections, online dating groups and sites, memberships, networking events, social outings, family or friend's introduction and unexpected encounters.

What type of relationships are happening nowadays?

The hook up culture is about temporary attachment. It is a disposable relationship model, often derived from a sex-based mentality, a trophy collection, a physical need to be met, a bounce-back or post-heartbreak behavior.

Friends with benefits help each other solve their personal issues without strings attached.

A boyfriend-girlfriend relationship is convenient and a mildly committal type of attachment.

Marriage equates to a long-term commitment. It is often the choice of the believers. It builds and strengthens real love. It means; I want to spend the rest of my life with you and officially take care of you in a blessed union.

A sacred union is multidimensional, deliberate, chosen, constructive and blossoming.

55/ RAISE A FAMILY

Earth living entities are reproductive beings.

Flowers, plants, trees, animals and humans are fruitful.

They all make up for the complete bio-ecological system of planet Earth.

Women are built to reproduce.

The physiological composition of a female body is built around the sacred womb, the milk creating breasts and the beautiful curves.

And the birth of a being is the most magical human experience.

The female system is based on hormones and cyclical periods that make her moody and variable.

The feminine character is strong, soft, enduring, loving, sensitive, emotional, heart-centered, caring, nurturing and motherly.

A man is physiologically built to complete the woman like two parts of a puzzle.

The male system has a solid physical body built.

Masculine mental faculties include strong will, discipline, problem solving, logical reasoning, pragmatism, effectiveness, competitiveness, action-based mindset with a mental ability to compartmentalize.

The man must be strong and able to rise and enter the female temple. The blood flow and the arousing leads to the union and in ovulation time, the competitive swimmers strive for one to reach the goal of fertilizing the egg.

Even nature duplicates the male and female model for fertilization.

The achievement of a willing woman is to be a mother and/or leave a legacy.

The pride of a willing man is to have a lineage and/or a legacy.

Now, free will means that humans decide to do what they wish with the cards they have been given. This is why we have recurring society trends, gender topics, sexual and behavioral choices.

In addition, lineage, childhood, education, lifestyle, culture, beliefs, life experience and past traumas have an impact on human life and thought process.

Finding the balance of masculine and feminine energy within oneself is key for harmony.

You think you are ready?

Imagining marriage easy?

Buckle and drive for synergy,
Face complexity undoubtedly!

                                          Couples spend years nurturing,
                                          A union of rollercoaster diving,

Spell enchanting love strikes,
Fit arrows of beloved likes,

                                          Dazzled eyes blaze light,
                                          Smiling hearts cry delight,

Both crave magic reunion,
Wild fireworks burst motion,

                                          Warm cocooning tenderness,
                                          Soften character sharpness,

Filled with hope and beauty,
Dreamed blossoming activity,

                    Spirits fuel electric moments,
                    Delights at birthing dividends,

Then time hits, hurdles and pains,
Mind screams hurt, body terrains,

                    Interferences and another third,
                    Disenchanting emotions blurred,

Expectations are shattered,
Is love real or just a word?

                    The lucky ones go smooth,
                    Constant honeymoon groove,

Some hiccup and start biting,

Some end up and face failing,

                                      A fatal blow of destruction,
                                      Souls need reconstruction,

Find yourself and reset,
Heart, body and mindset,

                                        Sincere hearts constancy,
                                      Rebuild tandem delicacy,

Fencing duo, dueling foes,
Evolve beyond inner egos,

                                      For a long-blessed union?
                                      God help and devotion,

Two to make it work,
Love duo framework,

The warfare of emotion,
Trial and error motion,

Temptations sideway,
Divert the right way,

Life throws challenge,
Take the risk, plunge,

What matters really?
Love romance worthy,

The bravery of union,
An eternal communion.

56/ NOURISH YOUR INNER CIRCLE

The notion of nourishment is to choose the right surroundings with people who positively feed your mind, body and soul.

Your family is an interconnection of blood ties that are part of your human experience. It includes your ancestry, genealogical tree and lineage network.

Your inner circle encompasses your family and social kindred.

Your network integrates your family and loved ones, your social acquaintances and your societal and business interactions.

Your soul connections are linked at a higher dimensional plane.

Human connection is a mutual exchange.

Relationships are enriched with love, care, appreciation, presence, trust, reliability, communication, gratefulness, understanding and support.

Nurturing relationships and maintaining ties of kinship help to build, maintain and grow your inner circle.

57/ PRACTICE MINDFULNESS

The mindful art of awakening,
Burst out of life conditioning,
Auto pilot mind switching,
Experience time breathing,

Cosmic dimension sensing,
Notice thought and feeling,
Emotional sense vibrating,
Divine energy resonating,

Rhythmic sounds are pulsing,
Mindful and conscious doing,
Mundane activity is playing,
Loved acts relish savoring,

Find time in busy day working,
Live the awesomeness of being,
Stirred senses experimenting,
Creative wonders exploring,

    From mind rambling to conscious thinking,
    From soul disconnect to oneness bonding,
    From heart aside to full throttle loving,
    Mindfulness is live and present being.

58/ HEAL YOUR WOUNDS

Healing is a process, a life experience awareness.

Who hasn't known crying?
Aftermath of heart-breaking,
Trauma, loss, commotion,
Or intense desperation,

Tears are shed in emotion,
A character, an interaction,
A journey, a site vibration,
An empathetic correlation,

Yes, we felt disarray,
When we lost our way,
Hurt, pain, betrayal,
Scarred heart abysmal,

The irony of rejection,
Say persistence in action,
Bounce back courage,
Face life with rage,

The lesson of hardship,
Take control of the ship,
Steer in the right direction,
Aim for reconstruction,

Continuum infinity,
A teaching polarity,
Sadness, happiness,
Life and death bless,

Sparkles first sight,
Abundance insight,
Love encompassing,

Healing & blessing,

Sure, we will be smiling,
Incredible heart beating,
Color palette in creation,
Magic geometry formation,

Are you not in awe?
An amazing life show,
Nature scenery intricate,
Awoken senses delectate,

The magic world beauty,
Charming constantly,
Aurora Borealis alight,
Starred sky at night,

I hear birds chatting,
Some insects visiting,

Many living species,
Fill eyes with stories,

The cosmical mystery,
The billions of galaxy,
From sky to deep sea,
Miracles, can you see?

Imagination boundless,
Mind thought endless,
Bypass the illusion,
Prompt exploration,

Miraculous creation,
Spiritual communion,
Scriptural correlating,
Dawn of new beginning.

As multidimensional beings, our healing must take place in all aspects of the being to be complete.

The impact of globalization, technology, portable communication, online lifestyle (AI evolution, news, video games, images, clips, movies, business portals, web and social media) and the covid crisis have caused a change in human thought and behavior.

Humanity has wounded,

Covid crisis was dreaded,

Face masks for breathing,

Small bubble socializing,

So much time indoors,
And struggling outdoors,
Relationships straining,
Online buzz thriving,

Tasting war times,

Curfews & confines,

Vaccines paranoia,

Irrational hysteria,

Depressed collective,
Now self-introspective,
Memorial for the dead,
Victims widespread,

Lesson of civilization,

Timely reconstruction,

Healing to revive,

Wellbeing alive.

Civilization symptoms may include the following aspects.

<u>Physical</u>: once identified, body ailments can usually be healed with care and medicine. Good habits, mental well-being, healthy diet and regular exercise influence good health.

<u>Mental</u>: subconscious and conscious memories, PTSD, depression, ADHD, etc. require self-awareness, medical attention and psychological resolution. Revising the mind with

affirmations, positive thinking, hope, guidance, constructive learning, self-discipline, focus and being mindful contribute to feeding the mind wellness.

Cognitive: ignorance can be replaced with education, seeking beneficial knowledge, goal setting and cleverness.

Communication: emojis, acronyms and instant messaging have truncated the linguistic format. Becoming eloquent, expressing your thoughts, ideas and feelings and communicating effectively are key for self-empowerment and positive human interactions.

Aesthetics: aesthetic evolution illustrates the quirkiness of modern society. Human standards in the realm of beauty, class, charm, allure, uniqueness, sublimeness, elegance, masterpiece, skilled craft and works of art often reflect its appreciation for forms, shapes, colors and textures.

Ethics: lack of ethics and morals can bring confusion if there is no referential benchmark. Possessing an ethical dimension refers to respecting and appreciating individual and collective human behavior.

Emotion: heartbreak, bereavement, stress, loss, grief, etc. are an inherent part of the life cycle. Acknowledging feelings, processing emotions timely, applying unconditional love and self-love contribute to the healing process.

Social: feelings of isolation, ostracization, loneliness, etc. are resolved with true friends, social outings, family support and community involvement.

Spiritual: soul disconnection, auto pilot mode, spiritual void, etc. are often healed with spirituality, faith, meditation, prayer, mindfulness and connection with nature.

> **Bible, Jeremiah 17.14** "Heal me, O Lord, and I shall be healed; save me, and I shall be saved, for you are my praise."

> **Bible, Psalm 147.3** "He heals the brokenhearted and binds up their wounds."

> **Bible, Jeremiah 33.6** "Behold, I will bring to it health and healing, and I will heal them and reveal to them abundance of prosperity and security."

59/ NURTURE YOUR AURA

Your aura is your electromagnetic field of energy.

Your distinctive energy blueprint includes all of you and what is stored within you: mind, body, heart, soul, cellular memories, surroundings, inner circle and core being.

There are seven aura categories:

1. <u>Etherical</u>: the skin touch layer, your physical health and fitness strength.
2. <u>Emotional</u>: all the emotions that you carry with you.
3. <u>Mental</u>: your thoughts, mindset and cognitive abilities.
4. <u>Astral</u>: love and bonding field.
5. <u>Etheric template</u>: psychic sensor that taps and connects to likewise energies.
6. <u>Celestial</u>: higher love, oneness, spiritual, enlightened, intuitive reading and dream level.
7. <u>Ketheric</u>: harmonizes all the above layers, soul level and guides to the divine path.

A spectrum of colors has been associated with auras and their variability reflects the current energy that arises from a being.

I think I saw an aura,

Light spectrum aurora,

Clear vision blurring,
Impression emitting,

Way beyond the visible,
A presence tangible,
Joy in laughter edible,
With heart incredible,

Pure love physical,
Interactive miracle,
Calm mind spoken,
Serene soul heaven,

Mindful educating,
Inner self-knowing,
True path connecting,
Divine realm entering.

60/ EXPERIENCE DIVINE ENERGY

When we perceive beyond the 3D reality, we become aware of the energy arena that hosts matter. By doing so, you access the floating awareness field that feels like cosmic perfection.

Connecting to the source provides a higher level of sensorial well-being.

Divine awareness is energy at a high level of consciousness.

Pure consciousness is magnetizing bliss.

It is divine essence.

It brings complete fullness, oneness and supreme happiness.

It leads to intrinsic and esoteric knowledge with an expansive feel of the multidimensional reality.

Divine ecstatic energy,
Cosmic light symphony,
Beyond bliss euphoric,
O mysterious esoteric,

Enrapturing heavenly,

Soul extraordinary,
Satisfaction plethoric,
Eternity timing static,

                                        Energy radiancy,
                                        Ethereal delicacy,
                                        Cosmos epiphany,
                                        Spiritual infinity,

I am what I am,
The One God realm,
Alpha & Omega,
Eternity aura.

61/ HEAVENLY REALM

Divine energy is the source of heavenly space.

The heavenly realm is the inner dimension within thyself.

There is a dimension of divine kingdom within.

> **Bible Luke 17:20-21** Being asked by the Pharisees when the kingdom of God would come, he answered them, "The kingdom of God is not coming in ways that can be observed, nor will they say, 'Look, here it is!' or 'There!' for behold, the kingdom of God is in the midst of you/within you."

The scriptures emphasize that the creation of human being is in the likeness of God and filled with His spirit.

> **Quran, 15.29** So, when I have made him and have breathed into him of My Spirit, do ye fall down, prostrating yourselves unto him.
>
> **Bible, Job 33.4** The Spirit of God has made me, and the breath of the Almighty gives me life.

Bible, Genesis 1.27 So God created man in his own image, in the image of God he created him; male and female he created them.

Bible 1 Corinthians 6.19 Or do you not know that your body is a temple of the Holy Spirit within you, whom you have from God? You are not your own.

The notion of a heavenly realm encompasses eternity, serenity, abundance, bliss, fullness, completeness, oneness, certainty and omniscience.

62/ ABOUT MANIFESTATION

The trendy topic of manifestation has led to an avalanche of online gurus and experts teaching and sharing techniques.

Kahlil Gibran is recognized as the New Age spiritual with the bestseller 'The Prophet.'

Established names like Florence Scovel Shinn & Neville Goddard integrate New Age spirituality with an esoteric reading of the Biblical scriptures.

The modern movie 'The Secret' made popular the Law of Attraction principle and the like.

Successful figures wrote about and taught those principles; the likes of Napoleon Hill, Eckhart Tolle, Rhonda Byrne, Deepak Chopra, Joe Dispenza, Louise Hay, etc. just to name a few.

Religious texts are interpreted with the God concept as an entity to which humans pray and supplicate to.

New Age spirituality integrates the divine soul dimension within the human being. In fact, the idea of a multidimensional being aligns with the scriptural notion of human creation: God blowing His spirit into the first being Adam.

The God energy within the human is linked to the Divine Oneness (called Universe, the Source, God, Allah, Elohim, Elah, YHWH, ...)

The history of mankind has shown how humans evolve and constantly innovate. Humans think, invent and create non-living matter on Earth. They maintain species survival with reproduction.

The known aspect of creation within the human being is illustrated by the constant advance in science, technology, transportation, building, architecture, landscaping, machinery, etc.

The human thought process has a creative output, and the initial concept starts with imagination. The felt visualization and internalization of a process leads to its realization. Sensory reality is subjective to the perception of the thinker, and this is why inner work matters.

The mind and heart cohesion represents the real deal.

> **Bible, Proverbs 23.7** For as he thinks in his heart, so he is.

The energy of feeling the wish fulfilled precedes its reality and the scriptures confirm how a sincere prayer is heard and fulfilled.

> **Bible Mark 11.24** "Therefore I tell you, whatever you ask in prayer, believe that you have received it, and it will be yours."

Now, notice the tense of the verse (asking is in present tense, experience the feeling of having it-past and you will receive it –future)

Bible Matthew 7.7-11 "Ask and it will be given to you; seek and you will find; knock and the door will be opened to you."

Quran 2.186 "When my servants ask you concerning me, I am indeed close. I listen to the prayer of every suppliant when he calls on me."

Bible Jeremiah 33.3 "Call to me and I will answer you and tell you great and unsearchable things you do not know."

Bible David Psalms 20.4 "May he give you the desire of your heart and make all your plans succeed."

Manifestation is the process of manipulating energy.

The mind creates matter with conscious thinking and sensory feeling. As the subconscious mind does not distinguish between fantasy and reality, what you believe to be true matters.

The daily stream of thoughts can clutter the brain, hence the importance of thought filtering. Thoughts are amplified and magnetized by the required level of attention and emotional charge. The selected and persistent thought, that is emotionally empowered in an aligned being, becomes a reality.

The powerful saying 'What you focus on expands' emphasizes why it is worth dedicating time and attention to cultivating your own mindset.

In the busyness of the modern world and the constant call for distractions, mind clarity requires laser focus.

CONCLUSION

Character building is essential for self-empowerment and societal cohesion. It elevates human consciousness and enhances civilizations. The practice of self-reform is a methodology of inner transformation towards self-realization.

Character reform within the self is an integral transformative journey that leads to soul and heart resonance, attuned to mind and body synchronicity. The awareness of your being walks in the depths of the multidimensional world of creation.

The powerful 'Logos,'

In scriptural echoes,

Teaches the mind,

Heart, body sound,

The letters wrapping,

Are soul enveloping,

Read and hear,

The call is clear,

'I am what I am' is,

Heeds what it means.

Printed in Great Britain
by Amazon